The Island Normal

BRIAN JONES

The Island Normal

CARCANET NEW PRESS LIMITED

Acknowledgements are due to the editors of the following periodicals and anthologies, in which some of the poems included in this book were first published: *Sunday Times, London Magazine, Poetry South East, Bananas, Poetry Review, The Little Word Machine, PN Review, P.E.N. New Poems 1977-8*, and *Poetry Dimension 5*.

SBN 85635 340 X

First published in 1980 by
Carcanet New Press Limited
330 Corn Exchange Buildings
Manchester M4 3BG

The publisher acknowledges the financial assistance of
the Arts Council of Great Britain.

Printed in England by Billings, Guildford

CONTENTS

6

I.

The Island Normal

'. . . *place your hands on the sources of its ugliness* . . .'

Kropotkin

OVERNIGHT

Stopping somewhere in England at a place
nondescript, halfway to our intention,
we get a bed and garage the hot car,
lugging only the one white case upstairs
to a room we barely look at.
We eat what's here and pass no comment—
it's chance after all that we've alighted
between the poles of choice.
                              But look at her face
who carries plates to us and responds
to what must be a child howling somewhere
in whatever part is private in this house.
She also is smiling since it doesn't matter
but going from the room has all the swift
compulsion of the really trapped.
We glimpse again all those momentous wheres
we're always absent from, as when
the train unscheduled stops, or the tyre
flattens in an irrelevant street. But not
tonight the normal rate of jettison.
Later we lie actually studying a room—
someone's taste of paper and curtaining, someone's
odd aside of a landscape, raw, unframed;
restlessly sleepless on futile snags of question
who have come in from the night to feel exclusion.

THAT HOUSE

Remember that house. To what end
did all that brightness shine? A bitter
woman at a bland party, the man
digging out her yorkers, the worn
smiles, the dry dry sherry. And behind them
framed acres of English idyll, the totally
unhelpful Eastern smiling gods, the bronze
boy chalice-holders, the perfect tints.
Marvellous, the sweet fields Misery grazes
and is still Misery.

THE ISLAND NORMAL

So often we push off from it, bored stiff
by its rightness, taking ages to jettison
the blue prescription of its near-shore waters,
and in no time we know we've insufficient
stomach for the great swell, and our bark
is far from noble, and should we both
flop and disappear, few will remember, fewer mourn.
It's the getting back that's miraculous—
it's really miraculous: chartless, inept,
working only at the next swell, the next buffet of wind,
we're hopeless. Then up it heaves, the Island,
as if unanchored and full of compassion.
Back over that bay, its blues suddenly gorgeous,
stepping on to the jetty, the wood creaking,
we're primed, it feels, like Odysseus with marvels.
But since we've been nowhere, precisely Nowhere,
of all those quiet Normalists, who shore-based know
the obvious horrors of ocean, who will listen?

TOO LATE

All those old crap songs poking their heads
round the blind alleys we walk and wringing
the nearest thing to tears from these dry hearts.
The air of putrefaction when the bar raises
its Sunday voice in 'I'll take you home again
Kathleen' and we all wanting to drape our arms
round everybody's neck and say 'yes, that's how . . . '
and waking with gritty head on Monday reading
another child is dead with his plastic gun.
Forgive our trespasses. We have many trespasses.
We're all doing our worst down the wrong
road, and the crap songs like Little Nell's foul death
jerk our sickness weepy. Sirens are calling us,
miles-away, long-sailed-past, long-refused.
Achilles shagged Penthesilea when she was dead.
Rightly, we feel revulsion. We understand.

TURN-OFF

The bland endlessness of by-passes
where only the gauges move.
Down this withering stump of a stopped road
I drive to *be* somewhere

and find this:
a decrepit settlement
in a silt of dusk awaiting
nostalgic decoders with clipboards

and trace-machines,
where a defunct brewer
sheds his name from a pub wall
and a splintered sign

beheads two villages.
A woman passes hunched
hurrying a child as if
on the edge of curfew.

My radio shouts like a megaphone
the simplified sickness of currency
across a landscape flat as misery
where a buffeted late rose

swings its shiplight reds.
The battens are slammed in place
on the surviving myths:
the returning father,

the ripening smells of the big meal,
the soft excluding swish of curtains.
I am a visitor
to my own country

and the guide books
are out of date.
A lost foreign lorry
thumps past and is buried in black.

The rose plunges
distress lights. In its
vast doomed hold
clever children grapple with New Maths.

MINNIS BAY

The slow falling flat
of England itself: walk out a hundred yards
and the water still just tickles the navel.
So hard to swim. Thank god so hard to drown.
The sea is here a nursemaid for the children.
We all, the hundreds of us, lie facing inland
hunting the travelling sun.
There is nothing to do. Convalescents are horribly sent
like this to do nothing in vacant places.
The children are all right, with their gothic sand
and crisps and cola.
It's the adults—white and burning, saying nothing,
heads sloping down on the slope of England,
coated elaborately in French-named creams,
unsecret in their poses, imprisoned from each other—
who distress. So many so. All we can hear,
thinned tuneless by distance and crosscutting wind,
the thump thump of transistors feeding the heads.

END OF PIER

Its abrupt angled indifference to coast
took the mind's breath away,
though bright-as-paint lay soldiers oompahed
on it, and an enthusiast's midget train
took you nowhere and back. The turnstile
thwacked your bum as you entered, vulgar
as the tatty comic turns. The rickety
slot machines flickered Edwardian porn
or, never converted, thrust out hopeless tongues
for ancient big brown pennies. Down it
you quitted Sunday afternoons
for a sky like Hollywood
with your first sweetheart. Below, fathoms of fear
merely licked the tree-trunk legs. A float
bobbed. A weighted line hissed endlessly
aimed at the horizon.
                              First, the fewer
people. Then paint peeling
from unprofitable arcades. Then three supports
gorged by the sea in one night of storm.
Then the fire, and this calcined skeleton
seen at first light nibbled into the sky.
Only inland is left. We watch the notices
nailed up: how it's forbidden to walk
now towards the sun, or strut the sea.
A small 'if only'
has gone, a yearning, a huddled
discreet town's V sign at itself.

RETURN TO WASTEGROUND

A patina of fuel on half-size marguerites
and a Volvo showroom with a launching party:
wide-lapelled young men, their raspberry
and mustard wool ties tumescently knotted: the wives
nuzzling older influentials with their uplifts.
Once I stood here in a fair among limping
fairground music watching a ferris wheel
mine couple after couple from the dark earth
and saw a fox skulk among perimeter diesels,
slung low like a lizard between its shoulderblades
expecting hurt. Country on the edge of town
means we are coming. First the fox goes,
then the fair. The only cause for return
now is a Volvo. A sheer and satiny one
stands like a celebrity no one dare approach
at the heart of the party. It cuts me dead
front on with its blank and armoured face.

SUMMER SLIDES

click

Everywhere, music bleeds
from walls.
To escape, we gorge fried rice
in a hotel bedroom.

click

At Blists Hill
we compare postcards:
your Victorian green Corinthian columns,
my stunned wheel.

click

The picnickers rise
from their false-rustic tables.
There is so much more to see
now England's a museum.

click

A blue-tit's remarkable
in a bird-reserve.
Eighteen binoculars
trap it hugely.

click

George improves his land
with staked Pre-Raphaelite goats.
Down the road
a Self-Sufficiency Exhibition.

click

That road seemed
yearning to fly:
so many magpies
flat, raising a wing.

click

Wordsworth sat here.
The air cooled
god's green muscles.
We study maps.

click

'Was he playing
Beethoven? I know
it was a transistor, but
was he playing Beethoven?'

click

. . . as on a darkling plain.
No. It's a
twin-bed hotel room
between somewhere and home.

HOLIDAY REPORT

While you're not here
'gorgeously swamped by
green water, collecting
eggs' things do not
stop arriving. That idiot
grinder with SISORS on his
cart who claimed his girl
had been raped knocks for
blunt knives. The postman
snaps those mean brown envelopes
on to your mat. They thicken like
the leaves fallen round here.
Someone has just
halted bemused, hearing
that phone ring and ring
through your empty rooms. Thanks
for that blue-sky card. I note
your ecstasy and the lack
of address should I have need
under the 'good neighbour' scheme
to inform you of disaster.

INTER CITY

Occasional user,
I still expect Karenina
steam about the ankles
and the strops uncles

used for razors
dangling to open windows.
Nostalgia and literature:
corridors from which peer

faces seeking empty
compartments, the sway
of slow oversprung
carriages, heard birdsong,

long uneventful stops
at a string of Adlestrops,
whole afternoons of hot leather
simmering in Edwardian weather.

This is not that kind of train.
More like a plane
it makes decisions
for you. Compartments open

as you approach, and slide behind.
There are no windows to wind
or drop swiftly for buffets of air.
All places feel like nowhere.

I am helpless and sit still.
Like life, it takes us whether we will
or not. I remember old times
I never knew: a lady climbs

out to pluck a primrose
as the train slows.
A man bounces, dreaming lechery.
A place that fosters free

will, where a woman can stand
watching the passing features of the land
dissolve with speed, waiting for
the moment to fling outwards with the door.

HERE

This Saturday is the flute-player's:
the emanation of ancient hillsides
sensual and sly as the dead gods
enchants pennies on the steps of the closed bank

while a street away the clanking drills
replace a third time the pedestrian precinct
ruined by delivery vans and sneaky saloons.
The citizens hate the foreigners

on pillaging day-trips. In amateur
camaraderie the archaeologists
have two more days of dig and clipboard
before the pros move in with yellow

ironclad bulldozers. A grizzled
stentorian dares an argument
placarded with the Socialist Weekly
like the boy in Dickens who bit, and skirted

by all except the catholic pigeons
who eat anywhere. On Monday,
the cleansing of the streets, the collection
of cans and wrapping paper, while outside

the Offices a small competitive
queue jostles for licences:
fiddler, dancer, players of spoons and recorders.
No flute-player, who knows the odds.

ELSEWHERE

While the damned clamber one another's backs
up St Trophime towards the blest who blow
their New Orleans horns and stamp
broad feet upon the wall of space below

Spring primps the Alyscamps and carves in light
the international young camped in the square
plucking dull strings of peace and dressed
in the mottled remnants of some no-good war.

Angling a quick kill, mayfly tourist shops
stock sunflower prints and Gauguin-labelled beers
and endless shelves of bonsai chaises Van Gogh.
We half-search for a stall of plastic ears.

We half-search for the alley where he ran
flashing a razor. Arles is full of thrills.
To get here we left England where she was,
crossed valleys, rivers, villages, plains, hills.

THE SLAUGHTERHOUSE FOREMAN'S SON

The slaughterhouse became the abattoir
when my promoted father took to suits
and no longer in the evening brought back home
that cold hollow smell of opened animals
or fingernails delicately rimmed with blood—
coincident with my entering grammar school
noosed in a black and silver tie and hobbled
with itching grey socks to the knee. On Sundays
we walked stiffly together in our new success
and have never since that time said what we thought.
I relate, however, to those departing cows
munching at mud as if it were lush pasture
in the paltry acre attached to the windowless
square building, towards which when it's time
they're led, nodding yes yes to their fate.

THE SLAUGHTERHOUSE FOREMAN'S DAUGHTER

I can't forget the ice of his returning
kiss or the touch that slammed the bolt.
When he drew his belt in a notch
it was a prelude to hauling carcases.
My friends seem to have no jobs.
My lovers shower and become real with a scotch.
When he carved meat, our table was silent.
My friends are words. He was hands.
In his anger he loomed in a blind room.
His caress drew my head swooningly back.

THE SLAUGHTERHOUSE FOREMAN'S WIFE

The heads lie till last,
he told me. Complete and watching.

The opened bodies I see them travel
wide and red as screams
losing the lapped kidneys
the livers bruised as afterbirths
while those perfect heads
gaze and gaze.

Only then the uprooting of tongues.
The scoop-out of brains that understood.

A SLAUGHTERER WATCHES

That brewery swallows coachloads whole
and spews them two hours later, pissed.
Floury barley, wrinkled dry
baked opiate-sweet hops, magical
sideshow vats of creeping yeast—
a tour of wholesomeness and splendours
ending in wayside pukes and hangovers.

If they came here, I'd make them leave clear-eyed,
with a dripping hunk, choppers, knives
and a bolted gun: process and product
indivisibly one.
Nobody visits. My children crawl
on graves for schoolwork, waxing dates and skulls
to decorate bedrooms.
I kiss them goodnight with work-chilled lips
and never stop to talk them off to sleep.

CAMBRIDGE: CLASS OF 19--

All gowned, and the gowns drawn tight
like sheathing wings of newly hatched
creatures before the spread of flight.
They seem assembled for some purpose more

than photographs. This one became
a small American death before
his work was finished on Hart Crane.
His doting mother brought him rugs and flowers.

This one, already lionised
by writers of repute, was last seen
licking the arses he despised
and vomiting on the London tube.

And this one versifies on northern heights
'shedding darkness on the gloom' as wrote
this other, two gowns to his right,
a neat-phrased critic who dreamed novels then.

Destined for business, medicine and law,
most of these others graze inside
fields where you don't ask what it's for,
expecting nothing from talent but success.

That is my own face. It stares
at the future as though it saw a ghost.
Out of shot, an apparatus prepares
to hone the best minds of the lost.

1976

Seemed undoubtedly summers had returned
and we to summers
                    Odd dislocation:
the honey-and-leather labourers
ransacking dustbowl fields beyond Sarre
faking another time until
a blue bikini flashed out or a yellow
Mediterranean sunhat

Pin-money operatives who were not there at sowing

And the white dresses across the lawns
and the picnics as though the page had never turned
and England hanging like a free fruit

The summer I read Chekov endlessly
parasols twisting in history-saddened hands
the gunshot in the decaying orangery

THE WINTER HARVESTERS

They crop cabbages, and edge
towards me, questioning the earth.
They do not speak. I hear voices
of whipped knife and creak of cabbage-heads.

It is wrong time. It is not my time.
The blind gape of the mouths, the raw hands,
animal-steam ghosting a strung herd.
They approach like something left behind

but dogging the route. Two faces raise,
cold, bitter, the human narrowed to
function like the blades in their chunk grip.
The sun slings from them nodding shadows.

One shadow does not move. The church spire
nails their slow line with a black transverse.
Years, through years they come, through generations,
forefathers battened to certainties

by Certainty. To stand in doubt
is to hear that slow pursuit, to know
the bequest still waits, when exhausted you
flounder bewildered, to seek you out.

CATHEDRAL

The Victorians set up these honey saints:
the vaporous smiles and mimsy languors
of a race that really put the boot in.
Our penury skeletons a steel unmanned
scaffold round the tower and waits for cash.
Inside, the Georgian ice-white elegant slabs
are cakes to sweeten death, and earlier
headless children wait with a headless mother.

Our scars. Our idiocies. Only this high
wing of darkness between stone and stone
flies out of reach of custom. Once, my son
with a six-year's terrifying intuition
hugged a pillar and nailed his feet with gaze.
You can otherwise squinny at heraldic nubs
and grip aesthetics like a charm.

OF GODS

Little remains of the gnawed man
With drugs stunned.
What was once painless is now pain—
Lowered foot, wrist turned.

Every morning the priest comes,
Enquiry the same:
'How are we, my son?'
'Father, we're fine.'

Other patients pause.
Godless debris
They're drawn to these
Men talking of 'we'

As if a man with cancer
Has a god, pain-thinned,
And the priest-comforter
The same god, concerned;

Then sit on their far beds,
Withdrawn, alone,
Who know that some gods
Die before men.

CHURCH

Here is the cliff-face of arrest
where good and mild and profligate
founder to a name and date.
The chill comes off the stone like breath,

and not the cross, or altar spread
white, or words declaimed and sung
engender awe like these who once
were human, and are simply dead.

Lovable now that champion
rose-grower, full-blown once with pride,
intolerable; and tender-sad
that brute imperial soldier, done

to death with spear-thrusts by a quaint
and vanished tribe he helped destroy;
and side by side the lovers lie
harmonious, perfect, as they weren't.

Engender awe: we do not know
how this heart-beat, this thinking sphere
can cross from Here to whatever There
is, although the one thing sure.

We do not understand, but stay
gazing at the names of dust:
the millions who outmillion us,
the heroes who have dared to die.

RUINED ABBEY

Indistinguishable dusk and rain.
The small-hut watchman
who breathes transistor and collects
pence has gone

and we're here for free
making sense of rubble
vaulting the stumps of colonnades
hanging the bells

two of the kind
that boots the god out like a bad landlord
and invents graves for the long-
dead tenants,

Melitus, Justus, whose stark soft
names score recent stones
above probably empty earth.
We move at a whisper

past where a king first
dismantled a wall
to lodge a mistress,
where burghers' carts

creaked off with quarried
blocks, through space where shepherds
penned flocks,
boozed, wenched, retched,

through echoes of men
who breathed faith like air
or raised faith like an umbrella
when they woke to repent.

Among ruins of hymns, laughter,
we wander: shades
with no home to go to
the morning after.

VISIT TO THE CHOUGHS

First, the English crows:
great purposes at dusk
flapping fullfed towards
the black roosts of the outcrop woods.

Hours then of nothing. Only
the headlights rattling white against
rows of trees, or spotting
a lonely house suddenly aghast,

until dawn and the Welsh roads
and ravens scouring the night-refuse:
blood-rimmed mats of hedgehog,
burst rabbit, spilt fox. Finally

this sunstruck littoral slope
at noon, and two choughs dancing
to mate on extinction's edge
beside the Atlantic's eery calm,

dancing on thin blood-veins of legs,
bobbing delicate bills, waving
the black wings that so sensitively
fingered our watching into recognition.

A ritual, fertile with oblivion,
a lively face-to-face that time will stiffen
into devices for a coat-of-arms.
Their tougher confreres mop up neighbouring farms,

launch themselves, and banner towards the sea.
We glance inland towards that moving host
whose beaks are door-wedges, whose claws
are roots for claiming and for sticking fast.

SUMMER: A KENT VILLAGE

Fat months: the Sundays swoon like Elgar.
We come here in their trance. The road
still like its root of foot-track
curves and the white wood still leans over.
An unemphatic church grows among trees.
A barn is blistered and loves its nests.
There's the rot of ancient masteries:
the gabled fine house and the great
vicarage staking the boundaries. A piddling
stream barely makes it under the bridge.
The neighing voice of a new villager
brasses the air. Rehash and reminiscence
stutter under his hammer, flow
from his brush and through the windows shine.
The distant roads are humming like winds,
singing like a threat that will break through.
Truculent, a man nails a high fence
and stares at us like approaching weather.

AT SHOREHAM

We've learnt nothing. Palmer tracked
diminishing moons through half of Europe
to sit at last in a redbrick stifled villa
in a room cluttered with forgotten lustres
while a Shoreham shepherd rotten at the lung
wheezed on the slopes of truth.
A vision is finally an open house
and survives when capacious.
Cars tilt nose-to-tail along the verges.
We clamour for an Eden whose gates clanged
forever ago. The walls of green
still startle sheer and close at the end of paths
but are just perspective. Behind them
men burned ricks and blundered in the dark
while Palmer's moon glowed on the orient corn.

CONFRONTATION

Palmer's self-portrait gazes straight through me.
Excluded from himself, his face
is a sac of unshed tears. A dying
lustre lights his forehead like a Shoreham
Palmer landscape. The eyes
are calling so that no one
else hears. The cropped
hair grains the way a blown
field flattens. He never knew
that what was done was enough. He lived
many years real as a wife to him
meaning nothing to us. Lunch was ready.
And the visitors' tea. And the intimate
cold-meat Sunday supper. A son
picked his way instinctively through the minefield
of a father's advice to an early grave.
The neighbours are cooking beef, lamb, chicken.
There's an hour of sherry before the sit-down stun.

INMATES

i *Newsreader*

That stub-rumped Citroen has all the pathos,
abandoned and slewed.
The small grey bodies lie at distance.
There are the weapons, home-made.
They could be from some gallery:
the art of dislocating the ordinary.
Soon they will see my face
controlledly weary with watching
years of disgrace.
I neaten papers at the end and smile
a priest-smile, doubtfully
proclaiming the possible.

ii *Dentist*

I mend their teeth.
They recline on my black soft
Clinicouch
rotten at soul, the lot.
I fidget decay out.
They spit and watch
and lean back sighing
as if it had been sin.
Can a priest do more?
An analyst?
Through whoever's door
they exit cleansed
already it's started again.

iii *The Poet's Mistress*

I see no reason I should ever
cast a shadow or see my face
in mirrors or water.
He and his poems

drew closer year by year
until with that brief
incandescence all admire
they coincided.
Then silence. An argument resolved
And Nothing made sense.

iv *The Boss's Secretary*

He chose the million dollar legs.
He told me that first Christmas at the dance.
The rest was easy.
I'm a tigress in a cage of gratitude.
I keep errors at bay.
He knows I make him invulnerable.
My mistake would be to let the truth in
or to gain weight or remind him of duty.
He knows that I know that he knows that I know
he's a turd.
If we must have leaders, let them go for good legs.

v *The Collector*

Chance
conversations, marginal notes
in books, instructions
for arcane skills:
my head
lumber-rooms from a mirror.
A Vergilian cobweb
sadness silvers all.
They've a mad glare.
A decamping's happened
leaving them their own meaning.
Gone, whatever climbed
the connecting stair.
Whatever spotlit
amazing usefulness.

vi *The President's Bodyguard*

I love the man the way he
put me to use. I was a bum kid.
There are thousands out there.
Hear the marble rap under my heel.
She don't give me lip now.
I got the pick She knows it.
I love the man the way we
walk and they hold off respectful.
We got it cleaned up and prosperous.
It'll end over my dead body.

REALPOLITIK

Now they drew near the Teutoburgian Wood
where Varus and his divisions lay unburied
after six years.

Caecina worked with his picked band of toughs
        laying the causeway
        planking with unbarked saplings
        the foul and obstructive marsh

while uneasy fires blistered the pig-meat
        and orders were given
to broach the finest and swiftest acting wine
and the officers instigated bawdy songs

At dawn the crossing
        iron clank leather creak
        no speech
        dulled heads not dull enough

into the full horror of expectation
        skulls nailed to trees
        horse-ribs meshing man-ribs
altars of turf for the torture of officers

A living army buried a dead
        weeping a furious pity
and Germanicus himself hurled the first earth
impulsively on the burial mound

'Let the grove resume
        its quiet roots
        the turf heal
Let Rome rest'

Back in Rome
it's said that Tiberius—for whom every
act of Germanicus was per se suspect—

laughed his cobs off:
to let an army *see* such a reverse!
for a commander belonging to the priesthood of the
                                                    Augurs
to *touch* the dead's effects!
Emperors store such rods for beating backs.

It came as no surprise when glamour-boy
perfect-spouse soldier-loved and emotional
Germanicus later let himself be poisoned
by a nonentity.
                        An Empire ritually mourned

FOOTNOTE TO A DECLINE AND FALL

Animal-tamers went out of business:
too proficient, they lost no hands to lions.
Not once in fifty years did an elephant's foot
topple from poise and crack a skull.
Safety-nets spared the spines of acrobats.
Their briefs and spangles became a tawdry glamour
glittering across the big top like stars
boringly safe in orbits. Stunt riders
were preserved from death by finicky legislation.
Singers mimed and no longer entertained
by forgetting notes and stumbling over words.
Soon it was all comedians. Two in particular:
the classically small and fat, the classically
lean, hypochondriac and smutty.
They pattered on, eyeing each other's crotch,
toupee and wallet. Don't worry, they said,
life *is* pathetic and dull. High art is crap.
Polysyllable is pretention. Your tool's too small.
You're ageing, useless, dull. We're *all* like that.
Sit on your arse and laugh at those who move.
There's only failure. Foreigners are fools.
Your wife's not what you wanted. We're with you, mate.
That's our arm round your shoulder. Listen.
Our jokes make everything petty, bearable.

The leading linguistic philosopher of the day
who later killed himself with a Greek knife
appeared for nothing on their show in a sketch
where he sat immobilised with the impossibility
of speech while they pranced in batlike
undergraduate gowns and mortarboards like teatrays.
A show which won a Golden Rose and clocked
an amazing twelve million on the viewing charts.

HER PARTY

And when the god is dead, who lives?
This conversation talks to itself.
That's Bach behind it, thick arithmetic.
Over the city a spire soars,
fount of aesthetic.

And what stays with friends gone?
Scummed coffee like walled horses' eyes.
Ash-trays brimmed with stubs
like visible lost time.
On glasses the shape of lips.

His lips torment me. How did he learn
such skills? His balls are tight. His breath
sweet. As he fills me I can hear
my guest leave. I've learnt tonight
Jon's queer,

Mary and Robin can't last
long. He's snoring and gone small.
Listen to those empty rooms.
How long since I slept
with quiet dreams

filled with faces I know?
Outside, all's silent, where
I laid a feast.
He's toppled sideways, sleeps like stone.
I'm my last guest.

HER TESTAMENT

All the fictions have failed.
I live here. Live now.
Only decay thrives.
A magpie drags its glamour like a target.
The outlandish is cut to size

as if Time were a kingdom
and that kingdom England:
its decrees faultlessly
enacted, love as
subject as a tree.

Once we shone
a thousand-year visitant
comet. Together
one. Now I hear
a logged bull roar

across the river in the farmer's
field who all day
breakfasts on scotch,
watches surveyors, wonders
what boating-rights fetch.

My paintings I've
burnt: love-letters
to myself they praised
the blue skies of my mind
my passion's July days

who prefer darkness now.
They will find me, my effects
lodged between head and feet,
rotten and cold.
No lavender deceits.

SUPPLEMENT STORY

She remained his housekeeper long after
the age of housekeepers and well into
the age of mistresses. He meanwhile
was extant among his dahlias, who once
espoused more subtle causes

although extinct to visitors. Latterly,
he's found himself awake, shouting
'Don't leave me!' The widowed causes
open their legs elsewhere. In her own room
she hears the cry. The old recurrent dream.

THE CITY'S CHIEF FIRE OFFICER

The City's Chief Fire Officer
is huffily this midnight drafting a memo
to the Magistrate to the effect
that the Community Centre, built

by the City Architect for an estate
designated an area of need
by the Planning Sub-Committee,
is a fire-hazard. He was not consulted.

He gazes in fury at the moon
where there can never be fires
and which prompts fires of love in other
breasts this night. He cannot understand

the irrelevance of his department to so many
kinds of existence. He is neglected.
His bendable lamp flicks down a cobra light
from its cowl. The pen his mother gave him

darts a pure vindictive black.
People never hang his warnings
in the right places. The world could die
of fire for all the notice they take of him.

He has all the forces
of water at his disposal.
He fears sleep like the future
where he is abolished and infernos dance.

REMEMBER REMEMBER:
5 November 1978

I pile first on scoured
ground sweet with bruised
roots of fruit and flowers
wads of this last year's news—

headlines, faces, snagging
the work: Ally MacLeod
caged in a ravaging
moment; a dead pope, tired

even in death, rictus
of failure now embalmed
in a million pictures;
'Midlands Typhoid Alarm',

then 'Typhoid Professor's
Death By Own Hand Verdict';
I note, remember, toss
page on to page, a twist

of each, like wringing necks,
then scatter dry twigs
over them, and erect
a chill structure of sticks

that cries out for a Guy,
some poor sod, some scapegoat,
to hang there, burning. I
wince as they stuff my coat.

FEARFUL

I'm a Romantic—it's just this unaccountable
agoraphobia that holds me back.
I'm a natural for footloose
speculation and shouldered haversack—

the expedition of one
among mistresses and orchids
though my whole sense of travel
is of life on the skids

plodding from chair to set
varying the channels
irked by endless reading
of minuscule novels

Why does space hate me?
The trigger somewhere and the finger curled.
When I was a child and real I lay
on our tar roof and itched for the world.

MR ELLIS

Mr Ellis, who continues
but does so little: my daughter
laughs at you among your
reeds. Uncleared fields
under a clearing sky. Can I
defend you, with my littered
papers and failed lines?
Three sheep-dogs, all untrained
and bewildered, and a great
shed of repeated rusted
tools. We do not know
your past. Like my daughter
you were very young. Like me
quite young. Was there some
dislocation, a moment when
a second pickaxe had to drop
beside the first, and the fulsome
foxglove lasted longer than usual
and grew like a habit? Look at her:
she beats the wet with her
bright new boots. One can forgive
failure, knowing it, but not
to children on a May morning.

MARCH THE TWENTY-FIRST

All the returning images. Farmsteads
glowing like old-brick braziers. A sumptuous cat
homed to a hot-spot, dozing. Cattle
crossing a field with that yes-yes of heads
as if earth murmured and they agreed.
We gather the brittle hazel the storms
long past shed, and later by the fire
remember walking the same lanes years ago.
Your hands smell of bark-flakes. Your hair
holds wood-smoke like a deliberate glamour.
To have strolled
so much nearer loss of each other
down lanes so little changed but for
that knowledge leaves me lying
hearing your deep sleep breathe
like steps departing, imagining
insupportable Springs—the wood-smoke
uncaptured, my mouth to kiss it gone.

WIDOWER

A melon-slice of beach. The heat
slung like a hammock between the headlands.
The sense that where we are is endless:
we never came, will never go away.
That's you in your burnt-orange swimsuit,
on an empty glisten the sea is fingering.
You perform the slightest of impromptu dances,
a shuffling skip of a street-game whose quick steps
still claim the child when there is no one by.
Night after night I crave other images
but dream always this. And when I approach
something like you is far out in a sea
that has withdrawn your footprints like a secret.

IN MEMORY

Taken out a lung-victim into the hills
two months off death still smoking himself to death
churning out dialectic
among the swaying grasses of the Malverns
dinosaur of the political steam-age wrapped
in Woodbine ash and fuelled
with original certainties

he conceded nothing to our wish
for an afternoon's evasion though we
maundered with beer and reminiscence:
the future is always death
of good men and always struggle
and the acres of astonishing green and rivers
have still to be earned.

We returned through dark in the coach
while he slept in a sickening depth.
The empties chattered in the crate like conversation.
A moon rose like something he had forgotten.
Now we must do without him—
that flame-like selflessness that exists to burn,
that must-maintain-this voice like larks over the Malverns.

NAIVE PAINTING

The cat-faced owls perch in the trees. The sheep
outcrop like boulders, utilitarian
and symbolic, with their martyred-aunt
skulls and humble shoulders. The shepherd
sprouts from the same root as his staff.
A russet housewife witch-brooms a baked
curved path. A child is learning with a doll.
The farmer's hands, as hundred-per-cent as pincers,
strap a dobbin to a red-wheeled cart.
The tree fruits as simply and as crammed
as intention. The brown track forks—right
to a sufficient store, left
to a wilderness awaiting the next
generation. Who dares to move
from these archaic postures? What time
is this? Where hangs a sun
so lavish and throwing no shadow?

IN MEMORY: E. S.

What kind of death is this we have to mourn?
For when I think of her I cannot mourn.
When lost in London, gripping her railings,
I wept and muttered This is the end
she opened her fusty backroom for me to sleep
and hung my jacket up and made me laugh.

She made us laugh when dutiful and taut
with dutiful taut family I visited her.
One night I dreamt of her and woke up laughing.
When relatives spoke of her it was with laughter.
When they shut her in a ward she had them laughing.
And now a small cortege creeps through the streets

she never left, and we look out seriously
on the battered houses she would not recognise
and the ones they've tarted with amnesiac white.
An old man stops and lifts his hat among
the crowd, and I thank him; and three children
to our amazement cross themselves and stand still.

Old warehouses blind with corrugated iron,
the road where she was born reduced to rubble,
her school a private house with BOYS and GIRLS
ghostly and chipped maintained as talking points.
And everywhere those bland discredited heights
stacked with people winkled out before her

who stuck like a last root in her basement flat
and would not go and died when they unearthed her.
What kind of deaths are these we have to mourn?
Old forms, old houses, old civilities;
three children's semaphore that no one soon
will comprehend? In dribbling music the unseen

fire turns you to ashes. You would have laughed,
laughed at the gibberish on the well-thumbed pages.
I cannot mourn for you, for you lived well.
Caged in your history and your class's history
you made the bars ring with your jaunty cheek
and cocky irreverence. I stand, and grip the railings,

gazing down. The door you opened for me is planked across.
Dead ice-plants shrivel against the boarded panes.
The first-floor workmen already smash the walls.
Bless you—forgive the word. Thank you for everything.
Old atheist-hypochondriac-anarchist, who knew
the world was crazy, embodied it, and laughed.

A SUNFLOWER OUT OF PLACE

Remember that water-meadow, once?
An old lady in a wide-brimmed hat,
up to her ears in willowherb, painting
very slowly, with clearly nowhere
else to have to get to? Why did we say
so little to each other about
a sight so marvellous? Rooted there,
she grew and flowered her yellow hat,
a sunflower out of place and still so right.

You are moving in sleep, restlessly.
We are at home, and I stare that woman
on to the small-hours' dark,
                        a traveller
beaming a slide-show to the oohs and ahs
of the institute of myself on a night out.

WOOD CARVER

The tap-taps nag like willpower, like a word
snapped at the wood—Give. Give.
She niggles a future from it,
worries it with a moralist's expertise.

Outside, the washed-out sea-town,
fashionable before there was Spain, blinks
some bleary neon and fills
tatty Rumpy bars with draughts. 'The facilities

are shit. Who cares about facilities.
Turner came here for the light and fell in love.
Palmer came here sometimes. They all came.
Van Gogh even, that lovely tender man.

Imagine it!' We hear the wind
spatter sea-grit against the panes.
The strip-light chinks and the room trembles.
'The sea threw up this wood. Thank God.

You know the price of oak now? The Japs
make cheap tools. If only they made cheap oak!'
I drink her Guinness and wait, and watch. Time
chinks the light and whips the wind. Her hand

withdraws. The wood has opened up an eye.
It's looking, peering perfect through itself.
A face is coming. A new face. It's a birth
from wreck. She breathes the eye bright like a god.

CONRAD AND NIGHT

'The affectations of irony and scepticism
have no place. After three days of waiting . . . '
I heap the grate with chicken-white split logs
and fail to sleep. There is nothing but black
and a fading scribble on it. 'He no longer dared
to think of Antonia. She had not survived.'
I rock before the flames in an Indian crouch.
I can't recall your face, or hers, or hers.
'After a night spent without even dozing off . . . '
The waste. To have let such lives slip. Such a love.
'The immense indifference of things . . . ' Countless
touchings and events accumulating
zero. A blanketed midnight dry-mouthed
zero stoking a heat and light
from a fire that yearns to die. Recite,
you said. Something you really know.
Recite it over and over. That's how I sleep.
' . . . whose glittering surface remained untroubled
by the fall . . . ' The dawn like the daily
paper crops up smelling new but
reassuringly the same.
'The sun lit up the sky behind the peaks . . . '
A crippled breast-stroke
heads for shore. Hopeless, but heads for shore.

ENTER SPRING

When the snows retreated
      and only pitted random corpses
of snow extended under the black
      glistening hawthorn

and the drake mallards whose heads
      shone fierily velvet in the renewing
sun butted the channels free
      through softening ice

and ghostly the squirrels with their slow
      moon-bounds plumed a looping smoke across
the convalescent air and lifted the dark-wet
      acorns from the leaf-rot

Came as every year lust
      of women and of far islands
and of life to crack like a pupa
      and stand wings trembling

'The feelings perpetual, but the thoughts
      of the age.' And there below in the valley
wavering behind the twig-fire the recurrent
      three-man picket

that has seen the snow out
      and the cocky wintering peewits
and the death of light at four
      and awaits the crocus

shoulders hunched and feet
      in a slow war dance against the cold
and on three faces wavy smiles
      creasing the heat-haze.

Down the ice came tinkle-and-gush
      and down in the woods the dead branches.
Down say the smiles since down it must
      come down let it come now.

ON THE EDGE

The arsehole of England. Muffled birdwatchers
squint through tears of windy joy—
ecstasy a puffball on stilts. A school
of local artists— acrylics and airless realisms—
endure the wonder of their admirers.
Remittance defectives, the trepanned crazed,
the obsessives abandoned to their treadmills,
line the seawall, blank as Aunt Sallys.
The Victorian towns crumble their piecrust
derivative splendours and are losing trade.
Decisions are made here. The word 'future'
bandied as if it were an option.

II.

Aeneas and After

Constitit et lacrimans 'quis iam locus' inquit 'Achate,
Quae regio in terris nostri non plena laboris?'

HORACE BIDS FAREWELL TO VERGIL

Odes I.iii

I trust, friend, you appreciate
the nervous cost to one who hates
the sea and loves late drink
of standing on the brink

while your unnecessary boat
drifts fainter in a queasy float
into liver-spotted mist.
A poet who's half-pissed

and whose tool and wit are frozen
can't deliver a few well-chosen
words, sublime or droll.
Vergil, you're half my soul

torn from me with slow pincers, but
just now it feels like half my gut.
And I know the signs: slow
sways the sea, no winds blow,

it's that dreadful act of balance which
the sea-god plays before his fits.
To trust a mind like yours
to canvas, rope and oars

and to sailors more hung-over
than I! O I see with horror
the nibbling fishes eat
you, anonymous meat!

I hold it truth a man with brains
should keep his hat on when it rains
avoid excessive sun
walk when the world says run,

and here you are, a luminary,
behaving like one supernumerary!
How will this fraught world fare
if poets, devil-may-care,

put everything at risk, like fools?
Poets, of all men, should know the rules.
How life is cobweb-frail,
to be spun where no gale

shakes it. How highest-fliers flop.
How hope evaporates like a dew-drop.
What most men learn with groans
poets know in their bones.

A poet's life and art should be
twin warriors against extremity.
(Excess of love and wine
permitted: both supine

in their aims, enjoyed at home,
they're free of the Icarus-syndrome.)
This urge to be away
when wisdom says stay

bodes ill both for your life and art.
The mist smells cruel. The salt is smart.
The blank sky has received
you wholly. I'm bereaved

and die your death. A double hurt.
O wandering soul, come safe to port.
And may we meet again
and drink and smile, and when

we exchange work, may your new verses
triumphantly mock my prognosis
and tell of one who found
home good, and tilled his ground.

AENEAS

1
A father prophetic among the dead
spells out the politics
of my inheritance. A wife
cries 'It is finished!' A palace
roars behind her like a hearth
grotesquely magnified. The lost
loved faces. The walled
city among its fields. My arms
encircle nothing and dare not let go.
Only
the burnt-out past is real. I move
on through sadness like wading water.

2
All point away. Tide and wind and prow.
And fate, in me reduced to history.
On watering-place islands
our fires of dead wood
sink rapidly to ash. 'Every fall'
I tell them ' is the future hoisting sail.
Lop the best trees to mast the ships
as the gods lopped Troy!'

3
Failure clings to us like a tradition.
A steersman overboard
welters from beach to beach.
My dreams hatch his cries for burial.
Every morning I must see to it
that my face comes up from bad dreams like the sun.

4 *At Carthage*
I come in out of horror to this warm bed.
Her thick gold hair murders the endless blue.
The sweet salt of her shoulder
is what the capricious ocean can shrink to.

When gods leave, fate pales to obligation—
a few sour colleagues waiting with twiddled thumbs—
somebody's books aren't straight—some letters
lie unopened—stocks are run down—a hand drums.

She does it properly. Her bed's exalted,
cornered with pillars, curtained with purple gloom.
Quickened with gratitude, I'm fully up to
the expectations of this sealed-off room.

At dawn, I wake alone. Are they still waiting?
Is that ship safe, banging against the quay?
Are we provided? Is that sail patched? Are
these the new gods—Detail? Banality?

5 *The Site of Rome*
A plain. Some mountains round.
A slowed river leaves silt.
A sow under the alders farrows
fulfilling prophecy.

The conspiracy of signs!
All this backslapping
and grins above the wine.
As if anguish ever earned

a simple future, and gods
grew never bored.
I bow my head
and whet stone a dull lance

expecting any time
a distant assembling clangour
our first harvest of packed
and hostile metal

at whose head
a young prince rides
so familiar: fierce
with love of country

who cannot countenance
thought of defeat or exile
whose wife waits in a walled
city for the only outcome.

Him I must track down
and with a joyous
savagery, that leaves my soldiers
stunned, nail and despoil.

AENEAS CONSIDERS THE TRIBES

I see these ancient fools worship their gods:
the one of gold dished in a roaring blue,
the other silver with a gaping mouth
singing in silence in a black surround.

Their opposition makes of one world two.
One god must fade before the other grows.
Allegiance cannot tolerate that both
reign unconcerned above a patch of ground.

My journeys are all sea in groans of wood.
Lucky the tiny islands, the hot coasts.
Lucky my journey should it come to good
poised over rocks. Beneath, always, the ghosts

crying from unshaped darkness far from land
claimed by quite other than the god they chose.
Our temples must house all gods, and to raise
them, men with ocean-tempered minds.

ON

There was one spoke of another journey:
the whole mistake
of keels pushed over shingle
into the blind sea

and squabbles about a new name.
Daily they watched him
farther and farther off
in that quietening corner of the room.

FIRSTFOOT

A shadow figure walked
into the wood beyond the settlement.

Behind, the deep drowse
of their first sleep

the bottles scattered
glinting like eyes

the start of walls
jagged against firelight.

The wood explored him.
He heard songs

die like a species
a crumbling silence of handiwork

the resentful slither of undergrowth
into the egg of another silence.

On the plains of the pitch black
the unkilled emerged gorging the unburied.

He felt himself
driven inward like a nail.

FIRSTFRUIT

At dawn
the women of the conquered

ringed the settlement.
By next dawn

the future had found its womb.
Delighted by relief

and a clutch of new tricks
the men

hewed rooftrees
and planked the sky.

PRESENCE

He heard another in the room.
The click of ankle-bones,

air through particular lips.
He knew he was himself alone.

He screwed the vice close every day.
But he heard another in the room.

TO SLEEP

He travelled to the beached ships
to scuttle nostalgia, the sweet dreams.

He saw the moving stones digest the planks.
A spine of keel

all that remained of travel.
The dreams ebbed

and he entered the mud-flat
sleep of absence

from which, reeking of landsweat,
he woke again, knowing he had dreamed.

A RELEASE

He fought for years. His body
closed in and tortured him.
The vice stomach. The gnawing genitals.
The ears were singing like a dried kettle.
The lungs cutting the air short.
He awoke from dreams coiled and whimpering.
He thrashed and squirmed and stabbed.
One night he fell. Down through the dreams
that cried for him, down through the roots of dreams.
He sank vanquished through water-table tears,
through the ooze of all decay, through the black
dismembering silence. It was the end
of all importance. Nobody knew
he had been born. The enormous flames
of an exploding planet quenched him painlessly.
It was sweet, sweet. He awoke laughing.

THE DREAM

He stood at the window
as the voice bade him.
He felt the air's affection

and saw sun misted
on a far hill.
A blackbird sang on a shining bough.

A stream trapped
a surprise of light.
Along a track

a man bore a mysterious load
towards a wood
whose trees fused

in darkness.
He closed his eyes
as the voice bade him

and knew the question
before it came. Is this
place dusk or dawn?

UPON CRAPPLETON HOUSE
The Beasts are by their Dens exprest   Marvell

1
And now, they said, there must be a Centre.
And they toiled three years.
Those who remembered proportions
drew thin blue plans

by night under cowled lamps.
The hefty wielded pickaxe
and shovel, gouging
troughs through strata.

The rogue toughs churned
mushes of concrete, and the more
precise laid level lines
of brick. And from the ranks

a plasterer came, and a strange
remote man with the secret of glass.
Out of the woods
chimed the strike of axes,

and, tall, fine-fingered, one
ruled and planed and stacked
sweet resinous planks.
Another, finicky, herringboned a floor.

And just as, in a hive
rolls a murmur, confused yet harmonious,
as creatures skilled in one skill
pursue their blind genetic stars

and miraculously the tiny
strictures of self merge
to elaborate concordance,
so the tappings, thuds, chink-chinks,

clanks, squeals and slithers
subsumed themselves at last
into the singing silence of completion.
And they stood back to see that it was good.

2
It was disastrous.
The high-hung concave dish urinals
splashed piss back accurately. The tiles,
pinned arsey-versey,

fell like leaves at the first big wind.
The elaborate concertina-sliding
partition slid once only,
jumped a crooked rail

and fell, scoring irreparably
a floor already found to be
susceptible to hard-soled shoes.
The elegant all-round clerestory,

lacking panes of like dimension,
made impossible the installation
of the cheap blackout required
for the inauguration of film-shows

envisaged to establish
the Centre as a place of pleasure.
The heating system irregularly
launched spasms of percussion

driving away a Yoga class that found
contemplation and the development
of inner harmony impossible
in such conditions.

No door
complied with the half-hour
burning specifications.
No cupboard was large enough.

No vision that they had of man
could be accommodated in
this bleak and bald
reverberating barn,

even the letters of whose name
sunk in a hunk of porage concrete
appeared slowly like slugs
only in rain.

3
Something had crossed
oceans with them,
tougher than nostalgia
or recurrent dreams.

So many leagues of emptiness
travelled, such pain
endured; and still incompetence
flowered from design.

The ashes were cold now
on that distant shore.
For this new beginning
they had come so far

to an earth untrammelled.
The journey stopped here.
And the Centre proclaimed
they had reached Nowhere

to gaze in horror
at their fresh start—
a Centre, sprung crooked
straight from the heart.

III.

At Great Tew

'. . . so that many came thither to study in a better air, finding all the books they could desire in his library and all the persons together whose company they could wish and not find in any other society.'

AT GREAT TEW
thinking of Cary, Viscount Falkland (1610-43)

' . . . and would passionately profess that the very agony of
the war took his sleep from him and would shortly break
his heart. He was weary of the times, he said, but would be
out of it ere night.'

i
As he could not heal his country's disease,
he longed for death. Dressing himself cleanly
as one going to a banquet, he drew the flap
and stepped into the tented field. An army
stirred, and small fires through the morning mist
blossomed. A nervous boy
fidgeted fingertips on the war drum.

He stands and gazes. The morning light
gathers like elegance at wrist and neck.
Across an English field he stares
into the mirror of an English field
where small fires blossom.
Between the fields, the dark fume of a hedge,
and a linking gap . . .

ii
High summer. The Cotswold stone
returns light, softened. Echoes,
echoes everywhere. The lane
tunnelling green through covertures of scents
leads to a mossed and pitted gate, beyond
which, becalmed now like a photograph,
his house stands, at whose table, before friends,
the wine and meat were sanctified
by ideals of moderation, while the candles
glimmered in Oxfordshire darkness, itself
in an England black with storm.
And the storm rose, and each light failed
one by one. No man survives

alone in blackness, can only grasp
whatever is to hand, and that always
is weapons, the simplicity
of alignment, leading inexorably
to a misty field at dawn
before the battle . . .

iii
Hooves
gather to thunder over mist-soft earth.
With light fixed in determined eyes
he kicks blood from his horse and pulls ahead
aimed at the mirrored enemy, that gap
clean in the hedge where image coincides
with image and a hail of lead. Comrades
and foes, stunned, rein back to admire
momently this career of death . . .

iv
The picnic crumbles, slips into the grass.
The Sunday paper brightly features
'suicide chic', the hagiography
of exemplary failures:
a poet toppling from a bridge,
an aviator heading out to sea.
The tone of commendation and the staring
ikons of centrality sit well
among advertisements which also fail
to mention price and efficacy . . .

v
The Sunday's camera would have caught it well:
that split astonished second when
two hell-bent forces faltered as there lay
between them a small island of one man;
until one side saw in the death
bravery flowering from a certain cause,
the other, panic from a loss of nerve,

and craning forward, screaming, both came on.

ANDREW MARVELL AWAITS HIS CHARGE
(In 1653, Marvell became tutor to Oliver Cromwell's ward)

The fountain spatters the stone boys.
An endless rainbow dribbles back
To sway the water-lilies. Poise
Is what the drizzling droplets lack

Then gain once more when thrust up high
By artifice to slide the groove
Ordained against this garden's sky.
The rainbow hovers there to prove

Art's function: how it can beget
From wasteful slop of water what
Is glittering yet is not wet.
For art is real and is not.

But art requires a sun. Although,
When clouds form, still the arc remains,
It is as grey as what below
Slips like decay into stone drains.

Blest are those peoples bathed in sun
Of certainties. Their simplest songs
Shine effortlessly and are one.
Eden must be where art belongs.

But now, unless one man can find
Within himself a grove of calm
Some quintessential spot of mind
Beneath disturbance and alarm,

All song will strain but to rehearse
The common wilderness where each
Is wandering alone. But worse.
It will be error granted speech.

About me, flower with flower chimes.
Colours concur. The beds of flowers
Like stanzas intricate with rhymes
Bespeak the quiet gardener's powers

Who constant among springs and falls
Handles each season's energy
Working on wildness between walls
To resurrect a harmony

While at my back an emptiness
Is by design of mortared stone
Shaped like a comfort from distress
To house the smaller house of bone.

For us, who cope with words, who know
The cries of butchered innocents
And how they pray who left them so,
The irony of reticence

Is all the crop we dare produce,
A tiny plot of sheltered green
Now wantonness is on the loose
To trample what is simply seen.

But there is one who spreads his arms
To welcome chaos of the times
Embodying all our alarms
And voicing nightmare without rhymes

Presumption I will not attempt.
My stanzas tremble but not yield.
To versify pride and contempt
Makes art compliant, like Mars' field.

He is a spirit great with powers
But here comes what he cannot see:
A tiny child among the flowers
Reluctantly to learn of me;

A ward of brutal times, and given
Into my charge, the future's seed.
The rainbow dances against heaven.
A covenant has been agreed.

The milkwhite flowers, the flowers red,
Tokens of innocence and pain,
Sway either side of his soft tread.
It is my duty to maintain

A tightrope discipline of mind,
My present to the future which
Approaches, nervous as a hind,
Green fields, or slaughter in a ditch.